Raising Big Heroes

Tips to raising healthy and confident children

Winifred Diete-Spiff

TABLE OF CONTENTS:

Dedication

I would like to dedicate this book to God, to aspiring and new parents, to the healthy upbringing of our future heros!

Basic Principles Of Successful Parenting

Raising and preparing your children may be the most difficult aspect of parenthood, and with reason. To have a pleasant journey, parenting takes delicacy, details, care, and understanding. Being a parent entails not only caring for the child but also ensuring that he develops properly, both physically and cognitively. Many parents have a variety of misunderstandings about parenthood that must be addressed permanently. This also includes parenting styles and methods. To dispel any misunderstandings, we will now discuss some fundamental ideas of effective parenthood and child-rearing.

What is Effective Parenting?

There are several parenting methods employed by different parents to help their children develop and become decent people. Effective parenting occurs when the child is able to focus on his or her work while also having the proper environment in which to flourish. Right parenting methods are usually beneficial in instilling effective parenting in people. Just going with your gut instinct isn't always the best thing to do, especially when it comes to fatherhood.

Good Parenting Principles

1. Do what is truly important.

Whether it's for your own or others' health, you must treat children in such a manner that they learn from you. The majority of individuals do not place a high value on acquiring excellent information in their early years of life. The majority of the students are engrossed in their phones, making it difficult for them to respond to the occasion. During parenthood, you must ensure that your children negotiate their gestation periods.

2. You can never have too much love.

Parents must strike a balance between their caring and severe sides. This is because being excessively affectionate might have a detrimental influence on your children. Your children may become stubborn or demanding. Your children can get putrefied if they are not given the appropriate amount of attention and roughness. There is always the possibility of charity, but don't make them expect you to love all the time.

3. Participate in your child's life

It is critical for you as a parent to set aside time to spend with your children. Being an active parent requires time and effort. You may need to rethink and adjust your priorities to maintain your children's health and priorities. Go out and play with them. Make them read a tale with you before going to bed. Inquire about their day and any conditioning they performed. This all affects their inside wellness and strengthens their relationship.

4. Create and Implement Well-Defined Rules

However, if you are not suited to handle this, it may cause you difficulties when he is learning and growing up in his adolescence. Try to make some ground rules for your children. It might be the moment of returning home, playing outside, going out with the Musketeers, or simply watching TV. All of these can affect their growth and gestation. As a result, they are more responsible and determined youngsters in their lives.

5. Encourage your children's independence.

Limiting their development and giving them a sense of control is vital. Limits, however, should not be so rigid that they impair their feeling of progress and freedom. As parents, you should let your children explore and learn from their surroundings. It teaches youngsters about tone direction. To be successful in life, you should raise your children to be self-sufficient, allowing them to chart their course.

6. Recognize Effort

You may encourage your child without always showering her with praise by being selective about the sort of praise you provide in the first place. To begin, commend her efforts, strategies, and success (e.g., "You worked well during the game!"). This communicates that impacts she can control — how frequently she practiced and studied for a test — help her reach her goals.

Avoid complimenting her for supposedly ingrained features that she cannot alter ("You're terrific at soccer!"). When she encounters a task and finds it difficult, her sense of self is threatened. Worse, she'll believe there's nothing she can do to help.

Don't forget to compliment her on her progress, not just the result. Cheer her on for not giving up on a mystification or for rehearsing longer to improve, not just for finishing a mystification or finally mastering a song.

7. Allow your youngster to struggle.

As parents, it may be difficult to witness our children suffer in any manner. We'd rather bone their food or fold their clothing than see them struggle with these activities (particularly when we can do them so quickly!). We intervene at the first indication of trouble and monitor every academy assignment.

However, constantly interfering limits them the opportunity to develop their accomplishments. When they've never had the opportunity to forget a library book or wash their dishes, they'll have fewer and fewer chances to learn to do so.

Yes, witnessing their struggle is sensitive and embarrassing, and you just want to wash their annoyance away. But commodity magic happens when we stand back and let them solve their difficulties. They acquire a new skill and, more significantly, they feel tremendously pleased with themselves.

8. Educate through illustration

Model the Behavior You Want Your Child to Display. You can educate yourself about anything - principles, habits, language, you name it. Do you want your child to spend less time on the computer and more time reading? Make reading a daily habit by reading a book in her company. Do you want her to keep her room clean? Do the same in your own space. And if you want to instill the same concepts and values in others, make sure you live them every day. She'll realize that beliefs and practices are passed down via families. They are so vital that everyone, including parents, follows them.

9. Maintain your cool.

When your child misbehaves, the most essential thing you can do is not to come up with an appropriate penalty or ensure that he understands his job. It is to be calm. Yes, even if he walked out mid-sentence and you didn't talk to him about his action.

When you're ready to discuss repercussions, connect it to his conscience without incorporating your annoyances. They should be founded on logical principles rather than fury. This also tells him that you're on his side since you're assisting him in managing his emotions and learning assignments without attempting to "win." ”

It's also appropriate to be adaptable, especially if you're ready to lose your cool. Some arguments aren't worth fighting because you'll later regret saying or doing something, or because your child won't take a bath this time (shamefaced!).

You are not required to punish or impose a penalty every time. You are not a failure for choosing to walk down if it means remaining cool and not becoming furious.

10. Do what works best for you.

Knitter whatever advice you get, whether from myself, other mothers, or musketeers, to fit you and your family. There is no better way to cares for your child more than how you do o
because you know him better than anyone else. Effective parenting isn't a one-size-fits-all recipe; what works for one (or several) may not work for you.

Yes, take the advice and give it a pass. However, filter information through the prism of what works best for your scenario.

11. Do what is truly important.

Whether it's for your own or others' health, you must treat children in such a manner that they learn from you. The majority of individuals do not place a high value on acquiring excellent information in their early years of life. The majority of the students are engrossed in their phones, making it difficult for them to respond to the occasion. During parenthood, you must ensure that your children negotiate their gestation periods.

12. You can never have too much love.

Parents must strike a balance between their caring and severe sides. This is because being excessively affectionate might have a detrimental influence on your children. Your children may become stubborn or demanding. Your children can get putrefied if they are not given the appropriate amount of attention and roughness. There is always the possibility of charity, but don't make them expect you to love all the time.

13. Participate in your child's life.

It is critical for you as a parent to set aside time to spend with your children. Being an active parent requires time and effort. You may need to rethink and adjust your priorities to maintain your children's health and priorities. Go out and play with them. Make them read a tale with you before going to bed. Inquire about their day and any conditioning they performed. This all affects their inside wellness and strengthens their relationship.

14. Adapt to the motherhood style

Various sorts of parental styles are engaged during a child's growth. When your child is growing, it's crucial to remember their age and adjust your methods accordingly. Saying no to a three-year-old is demotivating, but telling the same to a ten-year-old is necessary to make them understand the significance and worth. You must inquire about the appropriate classroom as well as social education for the youngster based on their intellectual development.

15. Create and Implement Well-Defined Rules

Still, if you are not suited to control such methods, it may cause you difficulties when he is learning and growing up in his adolescence. Make certain rules a part of your child while he is young; make some ground rules for your children. It might be the moment of returning home, playing outside, going out with playmates, or simply watching TV. All of these can affect their growth and character. As a result, they are more responsible and determined youngsters in their lives.

This practical parenting advice applies to a wide range of circumstances, from fussy eating to toilet training and beyond. For example, rather than attempting to modify your child's demeanor, accept it. Recognize the motive that inspired his actions before chastising. First and foremost, discuss sentiments with him so he may better communicate them.

Do not compare him to other children, as this causes unnecessary tension and anxiety. Demonstrate empathy so he knows you're on his side. Praise his difficulties, not his apparent ingrained bents. Allow him to suffer so he may understand how capable he is of overcoming hurdles.

You want to watch and educate by example. Focus on being cool before imposing punishments or tutoring a task. And, like with any great parenting advice, start with what works for you Because you know your family well.

These ideas have led and reminded many parents over the years, and I hope they might be beneficial to you as well.

A Good Beginning

Parenting Preparation

The process of preparation for parenting is divided into several steps, each of which provides its own set of obstacles and issues. Beginning with the decision to become a parent and proceeding through options for modes of delivery, the effect of new parenting, and child care difficulties, this chapter examines the phases of medication. Finally, the difficulties that parenting poses in a variety of less usual situations are discussed.

Preparing for parenthood begins with the choice to get pregnant or the unexpected discovery of pregnancy. Untrustworthy or unapproachable contraceptive methods proliferated in parenting for couples regardless of preparation. Furthermore, couples suffering from gravidity or multiple births had numerous alternatives and typically accepted their inability to conceive, eventually pursuing other parental options, such as relinquishment. The scarcity of efficient and consistent contraceptive and sterilization methods in recent decades has offered many people the opportunity to choose the time of their children's birth. Many couples with gravidity issues can now attain the desired gestation using advanced reproductive technology.

For some couples, the choice to become pregnant is carefully balanced against the influence that pregnancy and birth would have on their employment, cultures, financial position, and romantic relationship. Others look at the effects of pregnancy and parenting in isolation, or not at all. Despite a significant decrease in the prevalence of unwanted pregnancy among teenagers, council graduates, and obese women, the number of unexpected pregnancies among lesser educated, impoverished, and nonage women has climbed.

Birth and fertility rate statistics reveal fascinating labor tendencies. Historically, the birth rate of teens climbed at a 5-7% annual pace, culminating in 1990. Since then, the birth rate for teenagers has decreased by 34, a trend attributed to harmonious contraception use and detention in sexual exertion.2, 3 However, in 2006, the birth rate in the United States for teenagers aged 15 to 19 increased abruptly by3.4 travail among women 30 years of age and older has also shown an increase). The pursuit of greater education, jobs, and the need for two-income families have all played a role in the spectacular miracle of delayed labor.

Furthermore, all metrics of unattached labor have increased by 9 to 12 percent every year. In 2005, unmarried women accounted for 37 percent of all births in the United States. Nonmarital birth rates have recently increased, particularly among women aged 25 and older.

When Parenting Is Unplanned

Despite the scarcity of effective contraception methods, the incidence of unwanted pregnancies continues to rise. Colorful theories have suggested reasons for this miracle, including the intrapsychic conflict proposal, which presupposes unconscious solicitations to display fertility; and propositions of sophisticated contraceptive threat-taking gestation.

Adolescent pregnancy is a major societal issue, since the rate, which had been declining since 1991, increased in 2006. Parenting at a young age has an impact not only on the scholastic and social prospects of the adolescent mother but also on the babies born to teenage mothers.

As such, they are at risk for poor birth outcomes such as low birth weight and preterm birth. Research findings show that adolescent parents have high levels of stress, a lack of social support, a lack of understanding about child development, and unsatisfactory childrearing stations.

living at home with a parent or parents, the maturity of their children The capacity of adolescent parents to parent in a way that supports optimal child development is difficult to assess, and long-term studies are scarce.

While most teen pregnancies may be classified as unexpected, unplanned parenting in other age groups is more difficult to distinguish. The recent increase in unattached and nonmarital labor does not imply that the pregnancy was unplanned, as delayed labor and a concurrent rise in cohabitation render comparable figures meaningless.

Choice Of Single Parentage

Single parenthood has become increasingly respectable and fashionable during the last decade. Women who seek to become parents without the participation of a mate often fall into two categories: those who are dissatisfied with or bored with males in general, and those whose rising age demands them to become pregnant while they are still physiologically appropriate. For some, this constitutes an ethical quandary in which conventional family structures clash with the potential to make ultramodern reproductive alternatives, like artificial copulation, available to these women. There is considerable worry about the budgetary stability of optional single parents.

and a dearth of male role models for their children, claiming that these circumstances may deceive the child's social and cognitive development. Nonetheless, research shows that children raised by their mothers have better social and cognitive development and may have no negative impact on their matters. . Numerous reproductive drug clinics bear a cerebral profile to estimate the reasons driving the desire for alternative single parenthood.

Parents Who Are Gay Or Lesbian

Changes in attitudes among lesbian and gay men over the years have allowed many to contemplate the prospect of parenthood. Although some are contemplating retirement, the number of lesbians seeking artificial copulation and homosexual men seeking women to bear their kids is growing. Several businesses have been handled. Some may mistakenly assume that homosexual people cannot be excellent parents or that their children will not have adequate sexual role models because of biased views about lesbian and gay men that focus on their fornication rather than their specific qualities. Still, research suggests that the parent's sexual exposure has little influence on the child's sexual inclinations. Furthermore, gay and lesbian parents have been shown to provide effective parenthood for their children, and the children are not significantly different in terms of gender identity, personality problems, or cerebral development than children of heterosexual parents, larger longitudinal studies of same-sex parents, particularly gay men, are required.

Those concerned about the family's steady deterioration are defying these new, unusual family structures. Many institutions have cerebral webbing before being accepted into a patron copulation program. Gay males have fewer challenges since they must locate a lady willing to be inculcated and bear the pregnancy for them, or borrow. The question of legal guardianship arises. Although artificial copulation can reduce the legal guardianship battles that consanguineous lesbian parents must fight, the difficulty of changing a known patron or using a sperm bank presents a major problem. The legal, ethical, and health issues must be carefully considered by lesbian and gay men who want to become parents. Health-care professionals must understand these issues and be attentive to their specific stations about this type of ovulation.

Women With Physical Difficulties

A rising number of women with impairments are interested in getting pregnant and having children. Technological developments in adapted clothing and a rise in social assistance provide fewer opportunities for women with physical disabilities to consider pregnancy, labor, delivery, and childrearing. Women with functional impairments are more likely to be overweight, obese, have hypertension, and have internal health issues that hinder pregnancy. There has been very little research into the unique reproductive needs of women with disabilities. Evidence suggests that women with disabilities are more likely to have preterm and low birth weight babies, as well as additional sanitarium admissions during pregnancy, cesarean deliveries, and readmissions within 3 months of delivery. Recent journal papers have helped to increase the mindfulness of health care providers on specific issues. Health-care professionals and the general public must be educated to reduce the perceptions of helplessness and passivity. Sweats have been made to allow public access, and technology developments have given many women the opportunity to serve alone at work and home. Women with disabilities must consider the same financial and emotional aspects of parenting as non-disabled women. To make parenting a viable choice for these women, living situations may need to be modified, and a narrower variety of probative services is typically required. As a result, the financial cost of parenting may be lower, the initial problem more complicated, and the physical circumstances more difficult for these women than for women without disabilities.

Trends For The Future

Several cultural shifts have influenced parenting in the United States. Women are deferring labor and having fewer children. As time goes on, an increasing number of couples will have diminished fertility as a result of aging age. Conditions that impede a woman's capacity to conceive and bear children may become increasingly difficult to cure as she ages.

Additional Issues

More children than ever before are in the pool, and as a result, more children are in critical child-care settings. This is unlikely to alter, as two inflows are becoming less essential to fulfill ménage living expenditures. The effect of increasing the number of functioning maters is broad in scope. The number of necessary child-care settings will expand, raising concerns about their quality, size, and availability. Government authorities and companies must recognize the importance of big policy reforms to assist workers as well as their children. Birth attendants, delivery setting, parturition education programs, and colorful processes particularly presented during the birth itself are all options for women preparing for parturition. As women become more aware of their health care, the trend toward consumer engagement and control is expected to continue. To accommodate the needs of working women, wise healthcare practitioners and hospitals will stay up to date on consumer requests for bearing druthers.

Because of rising divorce rates, unexpected parenthood, and optional single motherhood, single-parent households are becoming more popular. Unusual parenthood arrangements selected by single professional women and homosexual couples are becoming increasingly common, testing social standards and redefining parental and family boundaries.

Having a child causes several changes in a person's life. Preparing for the transition to parenthood entails making adjustments in one's life and devising strategies to deal with such changes. New or pregnant parents, as well as others, should prepare for parenting by thinking about the chops, duties, and coffers that might help them become parents.

Many periods in life, such as pregnancy, parturition, and having a new baby, have a significant influence on someone. A new kid comes with new concerns, problems, and anxieties. It may, however, offer new passions, new understandings, and new manners. So, what should you do to prepare for parenthood?

Becoming A Successful Parent

Some say that being a parent is the most difficult job someone will ever have. It also appears to be the job where we are least prepared to begin. Having a child affects our life, and we must prepare for those changes. An expectant mother, for example, must learn about and prepare for the bodily changes she will experience during her pregnancy. Perhaps more crucial for individuals considering becoming parents is to consider and prepare for the internal and emotional changes or challenges that occur after a kid is born.

Having a child causes a variety of changes in the life of a mother or father. These transitions may be traumatic and exhausting. Some of the advantages of a kid joining a family are as follows:

• A child's oneness - Each baby is precious and unique. Parents may learn to appreciate each new word, small step, or endearing expression.

• Love's confines - The birth of a child provides parents with a whole new experience in love that may be profound and life-changing.

• Personal interests - While some new parents may have reservations, many parents come to feel more mature and responsible with a child. Raising a kid successfully provides a sense of accomplishment and significance.

• Sense of family - Children typically contribute to the formation of a new sense of family connection among family members.

• Specific development - Parenting provides the opportunity to guide, educate, and pass on values to the next generation.

• Parental closeness - Having a kid may assist new parents in understanding their parents' affection and opinions.

Furthermore, you may confront some developments that require you to undertake additional duties of the majority. Being financially responsible, providing direct care for your kid, altering part of your social activity, and managing motherhood and job responsibilities are examples of these.

The Function of Parenthood

Having a child entails taking on a new role in life. You may have performed the role of "parent" at some point in your life. What can we expect? How will it vary from being a "partner/mate," "student," or "worker"? When a child is born, you will notice that things are changing in your life. This may vary slightly for both men and women. The value of places associated with a sense of self will alter with the birth of a kid, according to research on becoming a parent. How do impacts shift?

Men and women were asked to explain how significant different places were to their sense of self before and after having children. After a kid is born, a person's "mate/partner" component decreases for both men and women. The "parent" element of a person increases dramatically for both men and women. The "worker/student" element of a person increases for men and decreases for women. This may differ for different men and women.

New parents should expect and plan for these changes in their lives and relationships. You might be spending considerably less time in the "worker" section and much more time in the "parent" section. Alternatively, you may find yourself permitting lower about your " partner " component while spending more time caring about your " parent " part. Allowing for the transfer to the role of parent, investigate two critical concerns.

What Are Your Plans As A Parent?

What adjustments do you plan to make in your life and relationships?

We may compare parenting to other careers. However, if you apply for a job, you will be expected to learn unique skills connected to the work. What skills are required for parenthood? What can you do to better prepare for the job? Exertion 2 can be used to investigate the process of preparing for the task of parenthood.

Allowing for the demands of this new job of parenthood may entail thinking about your role as a parent before and after the kid is born. What are the distinctions? Understanding once guests, certain strengths, and sources of knowledge that may help you prepare for the role of becoming a parent are also valuable.

Taking the time to understand the changes that occur in your life as a result of being a parent, as well as how to prepare yourself for parenting, may help to alleviate the tensions that come with being a parent. As with any journey, understanding where you want to go and how you want to perform in your new role as a parent can help decide the path you follow and the drugs you choose to achieve.

What Can I Do to Get Ready for Parenthood?

Then there are some essential assignments to review for your personal growth and development as a parent.

• Your concern over becoming a parent echoes how you'll deal with a child's torment. Children require a parent's tolerance and specific confidence. Consider yourself a parent, and work on your skills.

• Learn about child development so you may approach parenthood with positive and reasonable expectations for your child.

• Parenting gets delicate when you focus on the bad. Develop a good attitude about parenting and search for positive benefits to celebrate every day.

• Create habits that will continue over into your interactions with your kid, such as playing music, singing vocally, or chatting with your child.

• If you share parenthood with a spouse or mate, focus on developing a mutually beneficial connection with your companion and letting go of any anger.

• Expand your social support network as a new parent, including your partner, parents, relatives, musketeers, and so on. Learn who you may turn to for assistance, understanding, and advice.

• Seek appropriate medical assistance and social support if you are prone to depression or anxiety.

•Think about your once experiences. Take advantage of opportunities to learn beneficial methods of doing business if you had terrible experiences as a youngster, such as maltreatment or abuse.

• Read accessible resources or watch informative videos about preparing for parenting or caring for an energized child.

• Determine whether your local health department, hospital, or other parenting coffers or programs have trappings that bandy obtaining a parent in certain methods. Classes to assist you to prepare for a kid are typically offered by original healthcare programs.

Communication Secrets

We've all experienced how difficult it can be to communicate with children. They're still learning how to communicate, so they become irritated when we don't understand them or do what they want us to do politely. As a result, we as parents must be extremely nice and calm when speaking with them.

Communication with children and newborns is critical for their relationships and development; successful communication is listening to and speaking in ways that make youngsters feel important and appreciated. Talking well with youngsters assists them in developing skills for communicating with others.

Why is it vital to communicate with newborns and children?

Warm, kind and responsive communication helps newborns and toddlers feel safe and comfortable in their environments from birth. It also helps to create and deepen relationships between children and their parents and carers. Children require safety, security, and deep relationships to grow and acquire skills, therefore effective communication with children is critical to development.

What exactly is good communication with newborns and children?

- Giving your newborn or toddler your undivided attention when interacting with each other is an example of good communication.
- Enabling your kid to share their feelings with you and letting
- Listening to and responding sensitively to all types of reactions - not only pleasant ones or good news, but also rage, humiliation, grief, and fear
- Focusing on body language, tone, and words to truly comprehend what your kid is trying to say
- Utilizing your body language to demonstrate that you're interested in what your child wants to do with you
- Consider what your youngster can understand and how long they can focus.

You can promote and support healthy communication from infancy by talking to your child frequently and leaving pauses as if you were having a conversation. When the baby starts making noises and prattling, gabble back and wait for a response.

Tips for Improving Communication with Your Child

Working on creating effective communication skills with your child helps your youngster develop skills for talking with you and other people. It also strengthens your bond by communicating that you respect your child's studies and interests.

- ☐ Here are some ideas

Make time for conversing and listening to one another. Family reunions are an excellent opportunity to accomplish this.
When you and your child are communicating, turn off phones, laptops, and boxes. This demonstrates that you are completely focused on the transaction or discussion.
Talk about ordinary effects as you go about your day. However, if you and your kid are used to communicating frequently, it can make it easier to talk about huge or difficult matters.

Be open to discussing all types of emotions, including rage, joy, anger, fear, and worry. This assists your youngster in developing a "passions vocabulary." However, it is fashionable to wait until you have cooled down from strong emotions such as rage before discussing them.

Pay attention to your child's body language and attempt to respond to nonverbal cues as well. For example, 'You've been unusually silent this autumn. Were commodities present in the academy? '

Involve your child in conversations - it might be as easy as asking, "What do you think about that, Gabriel?"

Be ready to put down your work and listen to your youngster. You can't always predict when your child will start talking about something significant to them.

Tips for Active Listening with Children

Active listening is essential for effective communication and is beneficial to your connection with your child. This is because active listening shows your child that you are paying attention to and interested in them. It can also help you learn more about what's going on in your child's life.

- ☐ Then, here's how to engage your youngster in active listening.

Use your body language to demonstrate that you're paying attention. For example, face your kid and establish eye contact. However, if your youngster likes to talk while training, you may demonstrate your harkening by turning to gaze at them and being near them.

Pay attention to your child's facial expressions and body language. Harkening is more than just hearing words; it is also about attempting to grasp what those words mean.

Consider what your youngster is saying and show your attention by saying things like "Tell me more about." ', 'Seriously! ' and continue. '.

From time to time, repeat or rephrase what your youngster has stated. This alerts your youngster to the fact that you are harkening and allows you to double-check what your child is saying.

Try not to rush past, cut your youngster off, or complete rulings - especially if your child says something unusual or has difficulty balancing words.

Don't go right into problem-solving. Your youngster may just want you to hear and understand their interests and points of view.

Prompt your child to tell you how they feel by explaining how you think they feel - for example, "It seems like you felt left out when Felix wanted to play with those other kids at lunch." Be prepared to do this incorrectly, and ask your youngster to assist you.

When you teach your child how to be a good listener, you are also helping them develop their listening skills.

Encourage Your Youngster To Listen To Advice

Children usually require assistance in learning to hear, as well as gentle reminders about allowing others to speak. The following are some suggestions to assist your youngster to improve his or her listening skills.

Make an excellent component model. Your youngster learns to communicate by closely observing you. When you speak respectfully to your child (and others), you send a vital message about healthy communication.

Allow your youngster to finish speaking before responding. This is a fantastic example of harkening to your youngster.

Make use of words and concepts that your youngster will grasp. It might be difficult for your youngster to pay attention if they don't comprehend what you're saying.

Make any directions or requests as basic and clear as possible for your child's age and aptitude.

If you need to provide formative comments, send some positive messages at the same time. Your youngster is more likely to hear praise than criticism or criticism. 'You're normally very excellent at flashing back to put your lunchbox in the dishwasher,' for example. Could you please go back in time? '

Check out some additional strategies for better communication with your child. These suggestions might help you and your child communicate more effectively!

You understand the importance of excellent communication with your child as a good parent. Effective communication is critical for parenting children and preparing them to be responsible adults. It's not always simple to predict which communication styles will be most effective, but we've got some pointers to assist.

Hear Them Out

Making eye contact when talking is one of the most basic methods to demonstrate to our children that we want and expect them to hear when they interact with us. This implies that you keep an eye on harkening and create a landscape in which talk flows more fluidly since there is no need for frequent back-and-forth discourse about who should speak next.

Furthermore, active listening ensures that communication between you and your child remains as open as possible. A competent listener will grasp what a speaker is attempting to say without passing judgment.

This isn't always the case with youngsters who are still learning to talk. Once your child has mastered their language skills, you may begin practicing these approaches in exchanges with them as well.

Maintain An Open Mind.

It's important to remember that every tale has two sides and that sometimes both parents and children are to blame for a problem. In such instances, it is critical to identify solutions to resolve the issue without resorting to condemnation or judgment.

Occasionally, simply discussing how the impacts played out might help to completely fix the matter. However, in other circumstances, you may require the assistance of an expert, such as a schoolteacher or a family member who is not directly engaged with either party.

Furthermore, it is critical to teach your children that they should not place all of the blame on one individual since there are always two sides to every story. This is especially true if you believe they are not being truthful about what happened or if their viewpoint does not make sense for whatever reason.

By teaching them this at a young age, children will be able to avoid criticizing others and vice versa when difficulties emerge later in life.

Collect Your Research.

When you're worried about someone, it can be difficult to keep your sentiments and behaviors in check, especially if the youngster often expresses ideas that make no sense. Still, allowing yourself to process what's worrying you before reacting can assist ensure that your words are clear and avoid confusing or hurting someone.

Being furious when discussing a product isn't always a bad thing because everyone gets annoyed from time to time. Still, being cruel or unpleasant on purpose will not help anyone because they will surely doubt realize their error after hearing the bad feedback. As a result, many guardians refrain from speaking until they have completely cooled down.

Examine Your Tone.

When speaking to your children, you should always use a kind tone. Children may be sensitive, and they pick up on everything you say. However, if you scream at them or yell too loudly, it may have a bad influence on how they act around others.

Shouting also does not discipline because children do not process yelling in the same way that adults do.

Assume you need to educate them on a task; you must be strong and adopt a no-nonsense tone of voice that is explicit about what they did wrong and why it is unacceptable.

You should also explain how their actions harmed or affected others in some manner since this can help them grasp consequences better.

Make Eye Contact

Still, if your child doesn't establish eye contact with you or wanders around the room while chatting to you, it might feel impolite. They may be timid and distant, but if this is a recurring issue, talk to them about it so they understand why it's critical for everyone in the family and circle of musketeers to respect one another by paying attention when someone else talks.

When your child speaks to you, look them in the eyes so you understand what they're saying without asking for clarification. Kids tend to roam about when conversing with adults because there isn't much else going on at their position outside practice and TV time.

It also makes sense for children to check out from time to time, just as adults do, but don't allow them to feel down because they aren't paying attention when connecting with someone else, such as family members or musketeers.

Return To The Beginning

Children occasionally want or want distance, but parents have an innate impulse to assist and advise their children when they return home with concerns. Remember, not everyone has all the answers, so periodically going outside yourself and attempting to understand where your child is coming from will help you settle situations quickly.

When they're talking about their problem or dispute, don't passively listen by seesawing along, because your sprat probably wants someone to be there for support without you having to break everything for them. rather, laboriously hear, which includes repeating what you think they're saying and asking whether you're right.

At times, it may feel like a game of ping pong, but youngsters are continuously looking for opportunities to express themselves.

Make Use Of Positive Phrases.

Instead of using negative language or ambiguous terms like "do not" and "no," convey your desires appreciatively by employing verbs rather than nouns wherever feasible. For example, do not say, "Do not jump on the bed!" "; say, "Please take a seat on the bottom. ”

Try to educate youngsters on how you want them to bear from an early age, so they're scared of what's expected of them as they become older; knowing what their parents want of them now can avert countless difficulties later on.

Use open-ended inquiries that stimulate conversation rather than one-word replies such as 'yes' or 'no.' Don't offer instructions; instead, ask questions and provide options. This will teach children to think for themselves, which is a valuable ability that they will be able to utilize later in life when forming ideas.

There are several ways to be forceful without resorting to bad words or dictatorial methods.

Maintain Simplicity.

Keep your directions brief and straightforward. When communicating to young children, use simple vocabulary phrases rather than adult-sounding language; make effects simple for them to grasp.

Avoid using too many intricate rules that may confuse little children, but also avoid speaking too quickly, since this may make it difficult for them to follow the debate. Finally, make sure you don't forget essential facts like times or locations by writing them down somewhere visible so you don't have any trouble flashing back.

Give Authority

Giving your children a sense of control will make them feel more at ease, which will lead to more opportunities for communication. For example, if you want your sprat to take a bath, give him the choice of playing first before having a shower, so they know what's expected of them and can plan their day accordingly.

In this manner, they'll be aware of what's expected of them. You may also give your children options over their attire or meals throughout the day to give them a sense of control over their life.

Be Confident.

When conversing, adopt a forceful tone of voice to make both parties feel appreciated while still retaining strong listening skills to recognize when it's their moment to speak again.

Because toddlers have limited attention spans, you should avoid being ambiguous or generalizing. Your youngster must comprehend what has been stated by using plain language and focusing on the subject at hand rather than the various distractions common in everyday life.

Keep any interactions relevant, brief, and just bandy one subject at a time. It is critical to listen to what your child says since it demonstrates your interest in them and enables open dialogue with your child about their education and the topic of discussion.

Examine Your Comprehension

When interacting with your sprat, make sure they're engaged and harkening to you to see if they grasp what you're saying. You may also mention the child's name in your rulings and ask questions about their thoughts on a certain topic or present scenario.

Bonding

As any parent knows — or has been warned – adolescence may be the most challenging years for a child. Puberty, hormones, high school years, and developing demand for independence may be challenging for any parent. Every day in a family with an adolescent may feel like a war, often over insignificant issues. As a parent, you want to be able to love and lead your child in the same manner that you have always done, but you must acknowledge that as they develop, so must your connection with them.

Understand that teenagers' desire to spend more time with their pals is natural at this moment in their lives. However, it is still necessary to make an effort to spend quality time with your child now and then to stay informed about what is going on in their lives.

Keep your cool when things become hot; the only way to get your point across is to be strong and sensible. If you are too furious to speak adequately, you may always reschedule the talk for a later time. It offers you both more time to contemplate and concentrate on better knowing one other.

Make an effort to understand your child's interests and learn more about the friends who are significant to him or her. You will not only have a better understanding of your child's personality, but you will also have more possibilities to bond with each other.

The teenage years are confusing and demanding for both child and parent. They are, nevertheless, key molding years; the behaviors and habits your adolescent kid adopts now may affect their personality in the future and shape their character in the long term.

During this time, many parents are frustrated. Frequent confrontations may make you feel as if you're losing touch with your once-obedient youngster. However, you must recognize that your kids are most likely simply trying to figure out who they are and what they can live with and accept in themselves and others.

Things do not have to be difficult, and there are several methods for you and your child to maintain a good connection based on mutual respect and love. All you need to do is keep your cool and be patient while you adjust to the fact that your child is now a young adult.

Recognize Their Anxiety

We've all been adolescents; we understand the confusion and changes that come with the territory. We provide them with an outlet and a source of consolation when we attempt to comprehend their anguish. Most of the time, you will be able to connect to their problems and may be able to provide appropriate counsel to assist them.

Listen more than you talk; teenagers, like adults, want to be respected and listened to. Always be a "safe" and approachable person to whom your child may confide. That doesn't imply you have to embrace or agree with everything your adolescent says, but allowing them to talk freely (without interrupting) helps them to hear their thoughts expressed aloud. It also provides information on their problem-solving talents and limits.

Make Use of Your Own Experiences

Teenagers are in a unique era of their life when they are attempting to learn more about their surroundings and society. As kids acquire a rebellious tendency, this may get them in hot water with the authorities.

The last thing you should do in this scenario is pass judgment on your child. Instead, put yourself in their place; consider how you felt as a teenager and what helped you deal. Offer your youngster the same words of consolation that you needed as a teenager.

Technology Has the Potential to Be Your Friend

Teenagers now have access to considerably more information than any of us did while we were growing up, thanks to the internet. Social media sites such as Facebook, Twitter, Instagram, and others play key roles in your teen's life and are useful tools for keeping track of your teen's social movements and behavior. Learn to utilize these same tools to communicate with your teen in the same language and through the same media, and you will be able to build more bridges between yourself and your teen.

The Road to Respect is a Two-Way Street.

Nothing irritates parents more than a rude youngster. Set aside your parental pride and realize that respect is a two-way street, which will help you maintain a healthy family. Simple actions such as respecting their privacy, treating them as young adults, and accepting their decisions can help establish respect between you and your kids. Trust them and allow them to interact with their peers.

While you may disagree with their business, refrain from making comments about their friends. Instead, inquire about what they do together to encourage greater communication. Discuss the risks of indulging in dangerous or unhealthy activities and provide enjoyable alternatives. Invite their buddies to your home if at all feasible to learn more about them.

Maintain Your Cool

Take a few seconds now and again to remind yourself to be calm. When your adolescent acts inappropriately, it might be irritating, but threats and yelling battles will only make matters worse. Take a step back as an adult and consider what your youngster could have been trying to convey. Consider whether there was a point they were unable to articulate properly and devise strategies to help them communicate more effectively. If you find yourself losing your cool, choose to continue the conversation when you are more relaxed.

Demonstrate an Interest in Their Interests

Parents should take an active interest in their children's activities and learn more about their interests or hobbies. This is the most straightforward approach to showing your adolescent child that you care; it will also assist you both have more speaking possibilities.

Learn About Their Friends

Make an effort to learn more about your child's peers. Active participation in their social life can lead to improved ties between you and your adolescent. This allows you, as a parent, to speak with your children about their social lives. More significantly, you will know whether your children are socializing with the correct people, giving you better peace of mind when your adolescent is out.

Give Your Teen A Larger Role In The Family.

Being a member of a home entails more than just completing tasks or taking care of the house. It promotes a sense of ownership and responsibility. Include your teen in family talks and treat them as young adults with valid points of view. Encourage your adolescent to make their own rules and follow them.

Continue Speaking

Maintain regular communication with your adolescent. They may have thoughts that they are hesitant to share with their pals, and you may be the appropriate outlet for them. Again, draw on your experience as a teen to provide the guidance they require. You may not always need to be the one speaking in some instances. A sympathetic ear may be all they require.

Have A Good Time

When it comes to spending time with your adolescent, remember that quality always takes precedence over quantity. You don't have to spend every evening with your adolescent, but make time for a special supper or a day out to relax or enjoy their favorite activity. Try something new with your teen, such as fishing, seeking gourmet pleasures, or even competing in a video game. No matter their age, your child will undoubtedly appreciate the time spent and look forward to future activities.

Spending quality time together is a great approach to building your bond. Life may be chaotic, and the chaos can make many teens feel forgotten and alone. Making time in your busy schedule to spend time with a teen helps him or her feel important and appreciated. A modest gesture, like going on a stroll, having ice cream, or seeing a movie, can have a significant impact.

Establish Borders

Even if you have a young adult in the family, you are still the primary caregiver, and you must ensure that your kid understands that you are the one who establishes limits. You must firmly and gently highlight the significance of setting limits for your kid. Teens who lack boundaries may enter adulthood with a jumbled sense of having too much freedom.

Teenage years can be exhilarating, but they don't have to be a living nightmare. Regular conversations, excellent listening skills, and an understanding but firm demeanor can all aid in the formation of an unbreakable bond between parents and their teenagers.

Deciphering 'Silence'

Your child is a chatter bug — a talkative little bundle of energy — yet Junior is suddenly quieter. Perhaps your little princess is still chatty, but just when she wants to be. Even if your youngster isn't a "Chatty Carl or Cathy," but has suddenly reduced his or her conversational frequency, something is wrong. Why is your child remaining silent? There are no guarantees here but read on to discover whether any of these scenarios apply to your child and what you can do to get your child talking again.

Divorce and Conflict

My child is a talker, but after her father and I divorced, her chatter altered. She will joyfully speak a mile a minute, but then clam up when you ask her a question. My kid will refuse to answer even the most innocent of queries, such as "What do you want for dinner?" or the more emotional, "Are you sad?" She hears her father, myself, or whoever is asking her, but for some reason, she has decided to zip her lips at that specific time. This all started when my ex and I divorced. If you and your spouse are arguing, divorcing, or going through a trial separation, your child may opt to go on a quiet strike. It's difficult for a youngster to lose his or her family or to sense marital tension in the home, therefore not talking is a means of managing a situation in which your child has no influence! In this instance, your youngster may also begin to have accidents or refuse to eat.

What are your options? Well, I strongly recommend playing therapy because it provides a secure environment for children to express themselves, especially while dealing with family transitions. Getting irritated at your child for not speaking will not make him or she speak. It's incredibly irritating for my ex and me, so if there's a question she has to answer, like "What do you want to eat for dinner?" we'll press her or, if she refuses to respond, we'll make the decision ourselves. We frequently back off when asked a difficult question. For example, anytime I called my daughter to say good night while she was at her father's, she would frequently refuse to speak, and she would do the same for her father when she was with me. We discovered in therapy that my calling causes her unhappiness since it reminds her that I am not with her. I still contact her, of course, but we try to utilize Skype more than the phone since she responds better to see me and her father rather than just hearing our voices.

Adopted/New Sibling

Is there a new baby sibling in the house? It's exciting for your youngster, but learning to share the limelight is difficult. Furthermore, the new baby adds stress: weary parents, busy parents, prospective new babysitters, fewer playdates, less socialization with other children, and colder dinners! A youngster may believe that being silent is a good approach to deal with the changes brought on by a new sibling and to draw attention back to himself or herself.

What are your options? Because you can't send the new baby packing (and why would you?) try these strategies to assist your child to adjust to sharing the stage.

Use any child care assistance to acquire even an hour of alone time for the two of you. Your older child requires you just as much as the newborn.

Include your older sibling as an assistant. Can he or she keep the baby entertained while you cook? Can she fold your burp cloth? Can he help wash baby teethers or sing songs to calm the new baby? Make your older children feel indispensable to the baby's routine, and they will begin to feel special.

Recognize that your exhaustion has most likely made you grumpier than usual. Although your child may be too young to understand, addressing your child's complaints can go a long way. Please be patient! This too shall pass.

Bullying

When children are bullied, they are less likely to inform their parents. For an entire year throughout my middle school years, I was tortured and seldom said it to my mother, to whom I typically revealed everything. Even preschoolers, who are notorious for being brutally honest about everything ("Hey, look at that big guy" — how many 3-year-olds do you know have said that?) may be afraid to speak out about a classroom bully. Even if your youngster does tell you about a tiny old meanie, he may choose to remain silent on occasion.

First and foremost. Teach your youngster how to ignore a bully and make another buddy. We discussed it even when my kid was just two years old. The older a kid is, the simpler it is for her to do this, but discussing how to ignore and move away from bad conduct is an important lifelong lesson because bullies come in all ages and forms. Most bullies will avoid an uninterested or indifferent party.

Second, consult with the instructor and, if necessary, with the parents. This might be a problem if your child is of legal drinking age and is terrified of the implications of you speaking out. Only you, as the parent, can decide whether to let the kids "figure it out" or step in. If your child has been silent because of bullying, I believe it is a significant indication that the matter is severe and that you should act.

Abuse

Abuse, whether sexual, emotional, or physical, may cause anybody to shut down. If you have any doubts and your chatty youngster has gone silent, it's important to get the help of trusted instructors, family members, and a professional. It's as easy as that. Don't second-guess or question yourself: if your gut instinct tells you something is incorrect, listen to it.

Control, Fun, Or Simply Because!

For attention and control, a youngster may just stop talking. If your youngster is demanding attention and control, you must inquire as to why. Do you spend enough time with your child? Are you easily distracted or often on the phone? Perhaps your partner is too busy or works too many hours away from home, and your child is attempting to gain attention negatively.

Even yet, your child may be ignoring you for amusement or because he is too preoccupied with playing to respond! I can't tell you how many times my child feigned not to hear me because she didn't want to leave the park or use the restroom.

To get the ball back in your court, first, determine if it's because you've been too busy recently or because your youngster refuses to respond. If the former is the case, try to find a way to fit in some quality time. Because I share my child with my ex-husband, we will occasionally co sleep if I haven't seen her in a while. If it's the latter, such as Princess refusing to leave the park, recognize her sentiments, show empathy, and allow her another five minutes, but be sure to sound an alarm when the time runs out. Recognize, express empathy, and provide a warning. If it doesn't work, it's time for a punishment.

Remember that this, like other awful periods and phases, will pass, even if it is difficult. However, if your youngster becomes nearly completely deafeningly deafeningly deafeningly deafeningly deafeningly deafeningly deafening

The silent treatment gives your child the impression that he or she has power and influence over you. It's how they persuade you to leave them alone by pushing your buttons.

Know that if your child gives you the quiet treatment, it is most likely his greatest problem-solving technique at the time. Simply put, he's utilizing passive-aggressive behavior to cope with whatever situation is at hand. And by withholding facts or thoughts, he has gained the upper hand.

The difficult aspect for parents is that the more you make an issue of it and appear as though it is painful or irritating to you, the more your child will use it to get to you. And the less likely it is that your child will acquire more suitable problem-solving strategies.

Indeed, this style of passive-aggressive conduct may be quite damaging in later-life relationships. It's a pattern that you don't want to reinforce in your child.

Be mindful that if your child's quiet treatment is unexpected and unexplained, there may be an underlying abuse or medical concern. If your child is giving you the silent treatment, follow these six principles to persuade them to communicate and learn better methods to address problem

Rule Number One: *Don't Take It Personally*.

Many parents are offended by the quiet treatment. It is, after all, intended to make you feel helpless as a parent. And parents despise that sensation.

If you take the silent treatment personally, you may become frustrated and argue with your child. Do not attempt it. Fighting reduces you to your child's emotional level and teaches him that he has power over your emotions. Give your youngster no such authority. If you take the silent treatment personally, you may have to ask your child for them to be "nice" and talk to you. Don't do that again. It gives your child the wrong message. You don't want your youngster to learn that passive-aggressive conduct is a good method to achieve what he wants.

I feel that one of the things that children must learn as they mature is what their "proper size" is. Your child is the correct size since he is a human being. He is not a colossal being who can manipulate you by withholding your attention. If he's an adolescent, his appropriate size is that he's a teen dealing with issues that ten million other youngsters are dealing with. As a parent, your responsibility is to say: "We'll support you as much as we can, but don't blame us."

Rule Number 2: *Send a Clear Message to Your Child*

When your child gives you the quiet treatment, send him a clear message. What you should say is:

"Not replying to me will not fix your situation." I'll be there when you're ready to talk about it."

And now comes the crucial part:

"No cell phone use till then."

Or,

"No electronics till we talk."

Your youngster will have the motivation to discuss and fix the situation this way. And you're not putting any pressure on him. Go about your business once you've commented. Don't let it be a deal breaker or a roadblock. Believe me when I say that if you don't give the behavior power, you'll be far better off in the long term.

Rule Number 3: *Reach Out Only Twice and Then Leave Your Child Alone*

If your child is still not talking to you, I believe it is OK to check in and reach out to them. But be cautious. Once is most likely enough. Going to your youngster and begging him to speak gives him much too much power. It informs him that his quiet treatment is affecting you.

By the way, if your child suffers from silent treatment regularly, I recommend that you avoid reaching out at all. Simply tell him that his refusal to discuss isn't addressing his situation and that you'd love to chat with him when he's ready. And that you would keep his mobile phone till he is. Try to say this with a nice expression on your face. Remember that the expression on your face conveys a lot of your message to children. When my son was younger, I tried to wear an expression that suggested, "Everything's OK."

I never gave in to the impulse to shout at the group home where I worked with children with behavioral disorders. I'm not going to blame or point the finger at them. Regardless of how furious I was, I'd be as sweet as pie. I'd say:

"All right, we'll talk about it when you're ready." And no electronics until then. This will give you some breathing room. I'd then leave and wait for them to tell me when they were ready to talk. That way, I held power, but they could talk whenever they pleased.

Rule Number 4: *Motivate Your Child to Comply*

Here's the straightforward truth. It will die of neglect if you stop reacting to the quiet treatment. That is just what you desire. If it's not gratifying, kids will break out of the habit of freezing you out. And if they want to obtain something valuable back, they will talk. As a result, always provide them with a reason to cooperate.

In addition, if your child agrees to speak with you but then begins to object, tell him: "Look, if you're not prepared to sit down and discuss with me right now, let's not do it." Relax and wait till you're ready. But no electronics till then."

As a result, there is some motivation for your youngster to cooperate. You're also providing him with an option. Let's face it: your child will not agree with everything you do as a parent, even if you are acting in their best interests.

Rule Number 5: *Do Not Approach Your Child's Level*

Do not punish your child by responding to their quiet treatment with your silent treatment. Maintain open lines of communication with your child. When it comes to inappropriate behavior, I don't believe you should ever descend to your child's level. Don't respond to your child's inappropriate behavior with your inappropriate behavior. If your child screams at you, do not respond. And if your child refuses to communicate with you, do not refuse to communicate with him.

Remember, we don't want fights to start. And if one does start (which happens, we're not perfect), we want to get out as soon as possible. Getting down on your child's level nearly usually ends in a conflict. And you can't win when you're up against someone who has nothing to lose. You are essentially fighting with your child if you give him the silent treatment in response to his lack of communication.

Rule Number 6: *Make participation in family life mandatory.*

Adolescents go through a phase in which they develop a dislike for family life. And they demonstrate it. More well-behaved teens will be less vocal about it. They'll often shrug, roll their eyes, and say "whatever," not being confrontational or abusive, but also not engaging with you.

If you have a teenager who is acting inappropriately but still following the home rules, I propose that you leave it alone.

If you want everyone to come to dinner every night, make it a rule. I believe it's fantastic if your family can do it, but I recognize that many families can't. However, if you decide to have a sit-down dinner every Sunday, make sure your adolescent child is present. Expect them to stay for the duration of the meal. Let them sit there, make faces, and say "whatever." It doesn't matter. Just disregard that type of nonsense.

Again, you don't want to give those tiny bothersome behaviors power over you, or your kids will use them to attempt to press your buttons. If the conduct grows more irritating, speak with them about it personally. Give repercussions if they still don't cooperate. So if there's a family gathering, require your youngster to participate. Hold him accountable with an appropriate penalty if he is not courteous. It is his job to conduct himself accordingly. As a parent, you have the authority to compel him to do so.

Finally, if you don't give the silent treatment any power, your child will abandon it. It's not going to get him anywhere. When your youngster attempts to utilize it, coach, and instruct him by saying:

"Refusing to speak with me will not address your difficulties."

Finally, removing the power from your child's incorrect actions is the first and most crucial step toward assisting them in finding more suitable ones.

Managing Tantrums

When children experience temper tantrums, they may yell, become violent, or flee. Tantrums occur in young children when they are overwhelmed by powerful emotions. Tantrums may occur in older children because they have not yet learned safe ways to express or regulate their emotions. Talking about feelings with toddlers might help to decrease tantrums. Recognize children's feelings when they are having a tantrum. When the children are calm, work on emotion management.

What exactly are tantrums?

Tantrums come in a variety of forms and sizes. When your child 'loses it,' it can result in dramatic outbursts of rage, frustration, and disorganized behavior. Screaming, stiffening limbs, an arched back, kicking, falling, thrashing about, or running away are all possibilities. As part of a tantrum, children may hold their breath, vomit, smash items, or injure themselves or others.

Why do outbursts occur?

Tantrums are prevalent in youngsters aged one to three years. This is because young children are still in the early stages of social, emotional, and language development. They may become irritated because they are unable to convey their wants and feelings, including the desire to accomplish things for themselves. They're also learning that their actions have an impact on others. Tantrums are one way that young children express and control their emotions, as well as try to comprehend or influence what is going on around them.
Tantrums can occur in older children as well. This might be because they haven't learned safe ways to express or control their emotions.

Tantrums can be triggered by a variety of factors in both toddlers and older children, including:

- Temperament determines how quickly and powerfully children react to stressful situations or changes in their surroundings. Children who are more sensitive to these things may be more readily offended by them.

- Stress, hunger, tiredness, and overstimulation can all make it difficult for children to express and manage their emotions while remaining calm.

- Situations that children simply cannot handle, such as when an older child takes a toy away from a toddler.

- For youngsters, strong emotions such as anxiety, fear, embarrassment, and wrath can be overpowering. The ability to comprehend and regulate moods and reactions is referred to as self-regulation. It begins to develop in children around the age of 12 months. When something upsetting occurs, your child will be able to regulate their reactions and calm down as they grow older. As a result, there will be fewer tantrums.

How to Reduce the Probability of Tantrums

You can reduce the likelihood of tantrums by doing the following:

- Assist your child in comprehending their emotions. You may accomplish this from infancy by labeling feelings with words like 'happy, ' 'sad,' 'cross,' 'tired,' 'hungry,' and 'comfy.'

- Determine tantrum causes such as fatigue, hunger, concerns, fears, or overstimulation. You may be able to plan for certain circumstances and avoid the triggers, such as going shopping after your child has taken a sleep or eaten food.

- Encourage your child to pay attention to how they feel when they manage a challenging circumstance without throwing a tantrum. 'I just witnessed you build that tower again without getting angry when it toppled,' for example. How did that make you feel? Did you feel strong and at peace? ’

- When your youngster is quiet after a tantrum, discuss feelings. 'Did you chuck the toy because you were upset because it wasn't working?' What else could you possibly have done? ’

- Positive reactions to stress should be modeled. For example, 'I'm concerned that this traffic will cause us to be late.' 'Taking several deep breaths will help me stay calm.'

Tantrums are thrown by certain young toddlers who are still learning to talk because they are frustrated. Teaching your child essential word signs for terms like 'mad' or 'hungry' might assist until they learn the correct words to say.

How To Deal With Tantrums When They Occur

Tantrums do happen, no matter what you do to avoid them. When your child throws a tantrum, how you respond depends on his or her age:

- Time-in works wonderfully for toddlers; remain near, provide comfort, and tell youngsters that you understand their feelings.

- You may utilize 5 calming down stages for older children: recognize the emotion, name it, pause, assist your kid while they calm down, and address the issue that started the tantrum.

And the following suggestions may help tantrums pass more smoothly for everyone:

- Ascertain that your child and others in the vicinity are safe. If necessary, you may have to carry your child somewhere else.

- Once your kid is in a secure area, recognize the emotion they are expressing calmly - talk slowly and quietly.

- Continue to be quiet with your child until they settle down. If they want you to, touch or hold them, or offer them more physical space if they need it. Don't attempt to persuade your youngster.

- Consistently refuse to give in to requests. This will teach your youngster that tantrums do not bring them what they desire.

- Consider a 'paradoxical instruction.' This entails allowing your child to scream and yell until they are ready to quit. 'You can shout louder if you like,' for example. We're not bothering anyone in this large park.'

  When your youngster has calmed down, comfort them. Everyone is distressed by a tantrum.

Tantrums In Preschool And Early Elementary School-aged Children

Children at this age are also more aware that their actions have consequences. For example, when your child has calmed down from their tantrum, you may explain that throwing a tantrum is a natural result of other children not wanting to play with them.

If your child has special problems, such as autism, they may experience frequent or severe tantrums. See our page on problematic behavior in autistic children for more information, or seek guidance from the specialists who deal with your kid.

Managing Your Own Emotions When Dealing With Tantrums

If you can remain cool when your child is experiencing a tantrum, your youngster will see you as an example of calm behavior. Here are some suggestions for remaining calm and putting things into perspective during tantrums:

- Have a clear strategy for how you'll handle a tantrum in every setting. When the tantrum occurs, focus on putting your strategy into action.

- Accept that you cannot directly influence your child's emotions or behavior. You can only keep your child safe and manage their behavior so that tantrums do not occur in the future.

- Accept the fact that transformation takes time. Your child has a long way to go before tantrums are no longer an issue. Developing and practicing self-regulation skills is an ongoing process.

- Be wary of thinking your child is doing it on purpose or to annoy you. Children do not throw tantrums on purpose. They're stuck in a poor habit or can't deal with the circumstance right now.

- Maintain your sense of humor. But don't chuckle at the tantrum; doing so may attract your child's attention. It may also irritate your child if they believe you are laughing at them.

- Ignore anyone who gives you a filthy look. They've either never had children or have had children in the past and have forgotten what it's like.

- When things don't go as planned and a tantrum occurs, be kind to yourself. Raising children is a large and vital responsibility that all parents must learn as they go. You're giving it your all, but you can't control everything.

Emotions in Children

Children are little complex bundles of joy filled with so many emotions that are completely new to them. Sometimes they have trouble expressing these emotions, some have trouble with understanding them. This is where you come in as the nurturer, it is one of your many duties to help your child understand and express his or her emotions in the safest way!

Some Major Emotions to Discuss With Young Children

The various behaviors of your child are caused by a set of four complicated emotions. Here's how to explain them to your child in a way that he or she will understand so that they may learn to control them.

Children as young as one begin to express emotions, and whether you know it or not, that is when you begin to express them back. Remember when you told your child, "Ouchie," and scowled when he flung his toy car? That is an expression! By talking and showing them the proper approach, we implicitly identify, illustrate, and explain why our toddlers shouldn't act in a specific way. But we don't always take the same time and effort to provide emotional clues to school-aged children. If you just tell your child to go to her room when she misbehaves, you're passing up a chance to talk to her about why she misbehaved and how she might be feeling. These tiny actions can help your youngster comprehend the nuances of emotions by opening the door to conversation.

There is no school subject on identifying and explaining emotions, even though building and growing your child's emotional intelligence and emotional vocabulary should begin at a very young age, and it is as important in my opinion as learning numbers, letters, and color sorting. The function of feelings is to make sense of what's happening inside of us and around us. Feelings provide us rapid input to employ based on our prior experiences.

However, while you are young you have no past experiences to pull from—you react purely on how you feel. It's up to the parent or caregiver to instruct children in how to recognize, describe, interpret, and apply their emotions. Then kids will acquire a new language for self-expression. This language does not suffocate, shove down, repress, and then burst, but rather assists people in understanding why they are feeling the way they are. The capacity to experience, understand, and cope with emotions is the greatest gift you can offer your children—it will be their key to resilience later in life.

Rather than attempting to define a large array of feelings for your youngster, begin with the fundamentals. Here you will find the most prevalent complicated emotions from which all other emotions emerge, as well as how to discuss them with your children.

ANGER

Anger is defined as a strong sense of dissatisfaction, discontent, or animosity. Children, who are easily agitated when a playmate snatches their toy, become enraged because their fight or flight reflex is aroused. When your child screams, punches, or does anything improper, he is reacting to stimuli that have caused him to experience pain or frustration.

"Anger may appear unreasonable, but it's an instant natural reaction to some form of mistreatment your child experiences," explains Jaclyn Shlisky, Psy.D, a certified clinical psychologist on Long Island, New York. Because you know your child's conduct (his anger or hostility) stems from someplace, discuss it with him as it occurs.

Identify the emotion: Say, "It seems like you're incredibly irritated," and imitate the angry facial characteristics. It's critical not to use definitive words like "I see" over words like "It appears" or "It appears." According to studies, it is critical not to put exact words on an experience and invalidate your child's feelings if the child isn't mad, but rather sad or anxious. It offers the youngster the opportunity to correct the parents if they are wrong.

Explain the feeling: "Sometimes things don't go the way we want them to, and that makes us angry and unhappy," and then educate your child on how to express themselves when those feelings arise. Have your kid practice expressing something like, "I don't like it when you yank a toy out of my hand." According to studies, negative behaviors—hitting, shouting, or sobbing when angry—are the underlying emotion that has not yet been controlled or healed. A meltdown is an unacknowledged emotion—your child requires you to explain how they are feeling since they are unable to convey it themselves; this is referred to as developing your child's emotional vocabulary.

They need a word to associate with a feeling so they can use their words to express rather than react. When your child throws a tantrum, hits, or does something inappropriate, studies recommend asking them how they are feeling in addition to a consequence. They will understand that anger leads to hitting, and they will be able to express their anger in other ways. "*You have feelings, this is how they look, it's OK to feel, and no emotion is ever permanent*".

You should also do this on the other end of the spectrum: "*You just scored a soccer goal! How do you feel?*"

Making things easier: Pointing out emotions in others is a good technique for teaching children about emotions. "When you read story books or watch movies, ask your child how they think the character may be feeling. This not only increases emotional vocabulary, but it also teaches empathy, the act of putting oneself in another's shoes.

SADNESS

The feeling of loss, sorrow, or being let down is a major one for your kiddos. Sadness might come when your kid feels terrified, or when someone says or does something that feels awful. Sadness can be caused by missing someone (whether through death or distance) or having to endure something painful (like seeing your parents argue). Sadness can also emerge as a result of disappointment, such as early school closings owing to the coronavirus epidemic or a missed playdate.

When your child is upset, they not only feel sad, they think sad, and they will act sad. Tears are the most apparent indicator that your child is unhappy, but other signs of grief include aggression, isolation, and even clinginess.

By the age of one, newborns realize that their parents can help them manage their emotions; they scream, and you rush; as they grow out of infancy, toddlers begin to comprehend that various emotions are related to certain events. The risk of melancholy and failing to recognize its underlying cause is that sadness may evolve into a rage, which can lead to meltdowns. If you try to appease your child every time they cry, you're just putting a bandage on a problem rather than helping them solve it. Children need the tools to be able to say, "I feel terrible because..." otherwise they learn their feelings can be muted and they won't learn how to name the real reasons for their sadness."

Explain the emotion: For example, if your child loses their favorite stuffed animal and is unhappy, listen to them in any manner they need and show them by your actions that you are there for them if they need extra hugs, snuggles, or simply to weep. "You may also normalize their feelings by sharing a story about how you had a similar loss when you were their age. Be honest about how sad you were and how you cried. Talk about what helped you with your sad feelings is recommended by professionals.

Avoid the pitfall of saying "use your words" when a child is upset because it's not a reasonable expectation while the young child is still learning how to connect body and mind sensations with a feelings vocabulary. I tell a lot of parents to create a feelings chart using emojis—which all kids love—and use it to teach your kids to recognize how facial expressions correlate to feelings.

FEAR

Some fears are natural—most children are afraid of strangers, the dark, and separation from their parents—but having carefree days every day isn't the norm.

Identify the emotion: Because there are some fears we can't always protect our children from, such as a worldwide pandemic, validate your child's concerns about the situation ("That does sound scary") rather than downplaying how they're feeling by telling them everything will be fine. Be calm and matter-of-fact in your delivery so your child feels safe.

Explain the feeling: You can express that you have similar feelings ("I feel that way too") and ask your child if they want to ask you any questions about it. And if you don't know the answer? It's best to say you will find ways to learn more and get back to them with an answer. Sometimes simply allowing your child to verbally process what's going on in his head will help.

Making things easier: Because it is more difficult for young children to communicate the source of their anxiety, experts recommend telling tales, playing out scenarios, or reading books about a particularly unpleasant circumstance to help youngsters overcome concerns.

JEALOUSY

The green-eyed monster of jealousy has a way of getting the best of us, with it showing up in kids as young as 3 months, according to Francyne Zeltser, Psy.D., a psychologist in New York. It's an emotion easily felt and often expressed—mom holding a stranger's baby or a sibling getting presents for his birthday—but the concept of jealousy is difficult to explain. It might stem from a lack of trust and often leads to feelings of insecurity,

Identify the emotion: Jealousy and envy are closely similar; but, with envy, you desire what you never had, whereas, with jealousy, you are threatened with the loss of something you have or believe you have.

Material jealousy is envy ("I want what she has") that begins as early as toddlerhood. Toddlers don't think twice about stealing a toy from a playmate. Fortunately, once children are enrolled in school and begin to understand societal norms, they usually stop stealing what they want from their peers—but that doesn't stop them from wanting or yearning for the goods other kids have. Try to shift the focus away from material goods and onto the non-monetary riches your family provides.

Then there's **social jealousy**, which causes feelings of insecurity or inadequacy, such as if your daughter didn't get invited to a sleepover. Some children have an understanding of fairness that creates an inner struggle for them when a situation occurs that displays how something can be unfair.

Another type of jealousy in young children involves believing you will or have lost some affection, attention, or security from another person as a result of someone or something else, such as their interest in an activity that takes time away from you. This can manifest itself in the smallest of situations, such as when your child wants to have the biggest slice of birthday cake at his friend's party. Today, because it's your buddy's birthday, we're going to give it to him." Then, move the focus to something that will make your kid happy, such as telling your son to tell his friend how much fun he's having.

How to make things easier: The most common mistake parents make is telling their children, "There's no reason to be sad" or "Stop crying," which doesn't help the fact that your child is already sad; instead, you're restricting their emotions and telling them not to show it, rather than teaching them how to deal with it.

Emotional Understanding and Management:

Understanding and controlling emotions is critical for childhood and adolescent development. Children and teens who can understand and regulate their emotions are more likely to:

To recover from intense emotions such as disappointment, irritation, or enthusiasm, express emotions by speaking quietly or in acceptable ways such as impulse control, proper conduct, that is, in a way that does not harm other people, objects, or oneself

This is beneficial to children since it allows them to study, make friends, grow independent, and so on.

Understanding and managing emotions is an important part of your child's development. When your child is young, they'll need help understanding emotions. This mostly involves recognizing and naming emotions and lays the groundwork for managing emotions as your child grows. As your child grows, they'll learn more strategies to manage their emotions without your help.

Children Under The Age Of Three:
Children feel emotions before they can use words to describe them, and they comprehend language before they can use it, so you may assist your kid to understand what they're experiencing by helping them create 'emotional language. It may feel awkward to talk about feelings with

your child when they are still developing language abilities; here are some suggestions to help:

- When you notice your kid displaying an emotion, describe it to them and discuss it with them. For example, 'You have a huge smile on your face. You must be pleased to see me,' or 'You're weeping. You're upset because you can't play with the fish.'

- Label the feelings your kid observes in you and others, such as 'Auntie feels sad because she misses Grandpa.'

- Puppet play, singing, reading, and messy play are all good ways to help your kid explore his or her emotions via play.

- For very young children, big emotions like irritation, rage, and shame can be overpowering, and time-in can help them calm down and deal.

- Learning to comprehend and control emotions in children aged 3 to 8 years

- Children learn to recognize and identify emotions via practice, which is easier for them to do when they're calm or before their feelings get too severe. Here are some methods you can assist your kid in practice recognizing and naming emotions:

- Discuss the feelings that characters in novels, TV programs, or movies may be feeling, such as 'Look at Owner's face, he seems sad.'

- Try The Way I Feel by Janan Cain, All about Feelings by Usborne, or F is for Feelings by Goldie Millar and Lisa A. Berger to begin reading books on emotions with your kid.

- 'When I smashed that glass, I shouted pretty loudly; does that happen to you when you make a mistake and feel angry?' Help your kid understand how their body feels when they are feeling an emotion, such as, 'You seem frightened; do you have butterflies in your stomach?'

- Allow your kid to explore emotions through play; play ideas for preschoolers and play ideas for school-age emotions include messy play, drawing or painting, puppet play, dancing, and music play.

- Do emotions exercise with your child, in which you select an emotion, such as "enthusiastic," and play it out with your child, which you may convert into a simple guessing game.

- You may also begin teaching your child fundamental emotional management methods, such as:

- Teach your youngster techniques for dealing with powerful emotions, such as counting to ten or taking five deep breaths.

- Suggest methods to express strong emotions, such as clapping your hands when you're delighted, asking for a hug when you're sad, or squeezing your pillow tightly when you're furious.

- When your kid is upset, it may be difficult for them to apply these tactics; instead, they may yell, beat objects, or behave in other inappropriate ways, so you may need to help them calm down. Once calm, you can help them realize that strong emotions are OK, but bad behavior is not.

Strengthening Emotional Abilities In Pre-teens And Teenagers

Pre-teens and teenagers frequently experience strong and sometimes overwhelming emotions such as shame and humiliation; they may know the words for these emotions but have difficulty recognizing them when upset; and, due to teenage brain development, teenagers do not always have the skills to express and manage emotions in an adult manner.
That is why pre-teens and teenagers still require assistance in understanding and controlling emotions; but, with practice, your kid will be able to regulate their emotions without your assistance.

Here are some suggestions for improving your adolescent's capacity to comprehend and control emotions:

- Step in when you notice emotions rising; the sooner your child recognizes emotional shifts, the simpler it will be for them to maintain control over their behavior.
- 'When I was detained in traffic yesterday, my heart was beating and I felt incredibly hot; does that happen to you when you're frustrated?'

- Help your child recognize early indicators of intense emotions by saying things like, 'You're starting to pound that keyboard a little hard; might you need to pause for a minute and get some fresh air?'

- Discuss with your child what you do when you detect symptoms of strong emotions building up, such as, 'When I start to get extremely angry with myself, I focus on something I'm proud of instead. Would it work for you?'

- Work with your child to create a list of things they could do when they notice strong emotions building up, such as going for a run, listening to loud music on their headphones, or meditating; include as many options as possible so your child can choose the ones that feel right in different situations.

Remember that talking with teenagers about emotions won't be as effective when they're experiencing strong emotions; you must intervene early or wait until the emotion has passed. Our five steps to calming down for teenagers can help your teenage child manage emotions. When you work through this strategy with your child, you send the message that strong emotions are OK and that you understand what your child is going through.

Signs That Your Kid May Require Emotional Support

All children, especially younger children or youngsters dealing with additional obstacles such as a loss in the family or another traumatic incident, require aid and support to handle intense emotions at times. Children may require assistance in dealing with intense emotions if;

- They are unhappy or dissatisfied with how overwhelming their feelings are.
- They experience extremely intense emotions that are out of proportion to the problem or circumstance.
- They continue to have powerful emotions for a long time after whatever triggered the emotions.
- They frequently go from a peaceful state to extreme emotion, such as fury, in a matter of seconds.
- They incorrectly exhibit emotions, such as laughing in response to tragic news.
- When they are overwhelmed, they become very silent, hide, or push others away.

Also, pre-teen and adolescent children may require assistance if;

- They appear to make poor judgments because they are experiencing intense emotions such as frustration.
- They struggle to unwind sufficiently to enjoy their hobbies or spend time with family and friends.
- You can use the tips above to support your child whenever they experience strong emotions, but if you believe your child requires more help dealing with their emotions, talk to their GP first. The GP can help you find support for your child, which may include seeing a counselor or psychologist. A school counselor may also be able to assist.

Discipline and love

Discipline is teaching your kid how to behave as well as how not to behave, and it works best when you have a warm and caring relationship with your child. Discipline and discipline tactics are positive, based on talking and listening, and they steer children towards a few things such as;

- ☐ Knowing what is proper behavior, whether at home, a friend's house, child care, preschool, or school.

- ☐ Managing their behavior and acquiring crucial skills such as getting along with others

- ☐ Learning to recognize, control, and express their emotions.

Selecting an Effective Discipline Strategy

Choosing a disciplined approach is about finding the right balance; too little discipline can leave children feeling insecure and parents feeling out of control; too much negative discipline and not enough praise and rewards may result in children behaving well, but out of fear, which can lead to problems with children's self-esteem and anxiety later in life. When you establish boundaries and consequences for your child's behavior while simultaneously promoting good behavior with praise, prizes, and other tactics, discipline works best.

Your method of discipline will also be influenced by factors such as your parenting style, your child's developmental stage, and temperament.

Physical punishment, like slapping, does not teach children how to behave; when parents employ physical punishment, their children are more likely to exhibit problematic behavior, anxiety, or sadness, and there is also a chance that smacking will injure your kid.

Discipline At Various Ages

Discipline methods will vary based on what is happening for your child at various phases of development.

Babies

Babies do things to put their growing talents to the test, and they also like causing things to happen, such as when they yank your hair. However, newborns do not grasp consequences and do not recognize the difference between right and wrong. This indicates that negative consequences, such as punishment, are ineffective for newborns. Instead, newborns want warm, loving care to feel safe, so when your baby tugs your hair, you may say 'no' and show your baby how to gently touch your hair; you may need to do this several times because your baby may not remember from one time to the next.

Toddlers

Toddlers frequently struggle with strong emotions such as irritation and rage, since their social and emotional abilities are still developing, and they may be testing their emerging independence.

You may help your kid behave properly by paying attention to their feelings, altering the surroundings, diverting your child, and planning for difficult circumstances; our toddler behavior management ideas and tools discuss these and other disciplinary tactics.

Preschoolers

Most preschoolers begin to understand what is and isn't acceptable behavior around the age of three. They will test out different behaviors, and they may behave in certain ways more than once as they learn about consequences. You can help your preschooler by setting boundaries and being clear about the behavior you want to see. Our preschooler behavior management advice and resources provide information on adapting discipline tactics to your child's behavior.

Children Of School Age

School-age children may understand how to behave in various settings, such as school, home, or the library, but they still require you to remind them of the boundaries and reward them for good behavior. Most instructors in Australia have constructive skills for dealing with tough behavior in the classroom and on the playground, so speaking with your child's teacher is a good place to start if you're concerned about his or her behavior.

Discipline and better kid behavior are being implemented. Clearing behavioral expectations for your child are the cornerstone of discipline; here's how to get started.

1. Establish family rules.

Starting with 4-5 family rules is a good place to start, for example, your family rules may be:
We communicate effectively with one another.
We take care of others.
Everyone pitches in around the house.
We take care of our belongings.

Children as young as three years old can help you set the rules and explain why your family requires them.

2. Be a role model for the behavior you want to see.

Children learn by observing what you do, therefore modeling the behavior you want in your kid by doing it yourself, for example, if you want your child to sit down to eat, sitting down together to eat family meals can assist children to acquire this behavior.

3. Reward your youngster for good behavior.

Praise is when you tell your child what you admire about them or their behavior, and when your child receives praise for behaving well, he or she is more likely to want to continue behaving well.

Descriptive praise is used to encourage positive behavior by telling your child exactly what you admire. For example, 'Ali, I enjoy how you used please and thank you just now. Great manners!'

4. Establish clear boundaries and punishments

Decide on punishment for breaching a family rule; for example, if your 8-year-old hasn't done their home tasks, the punishment may be a week's worth of pocket money. When you employ penalties consistently and for the same behavior, your child learns what to anticipate.

Increasing Your Child's Confidence

As children get older, that confidence may become as vital as the skills themselves. To succeed, children must have faith in their talents while also understanding that they can endure failure. They build healthy self-confidence through experiencing mastery and recovering from failure.

Here are 12 strategies to help youngsters feel capable and get the most out of their abilities and talents.

1. Be an example of self-assurance.

Even if you're not feeling it! Seeing you approach new responsibilities with optimism and lots of preparation provides a fantastic example for children. That doesn't mean you have to pretend to be perfect; admit your worry, but don't dwell on it; instead, focus on the positive things you're doing to prepare.

2. Do not get offended by blunders.

Help children understand that everyone makes mistakes and that the essential thing is to learn from them rather than dwell on them. Confident individuals don't allow fear of failure to hold them back—not because they're certain they'll never fail, but because they know how to deal with setbacks.

3. Encourage them to experiment with new things.

Rather than spending all of their efforts on what they currently excel at, it is beneficial for children to diversify; learning new abilities lets them feel capable and confident that they can handle whatever comes their way.

4. Allow children to fail

It's natural to want to shield your child from failure, but trial and error are how children learn, and falling short of a goal teaches children that failure is not deadly, and it may also motivate them to work harder as adults.

5. Recognize persistence

Learning not to quit after the first failure or to bail after one setback is a crucial life skill. Confidence and self-esteem are about being tough enough to keep trying and not getting disturbed if you're not the greatest.

6. Assist children in discovering their interest

Exploring their hobbies may help children establish a sense of identity, which is crucial for confidence development, and watching their abilities flourish can also increase their self-esteem.

7. Establish objectives

Helping your child turn desires and dreams into actionable goals by encouraging them to make a list of things they'd like to accomplish, then practice breaking down longer-term goals into realistic benchmarks. You'll be validating their interests and helping them learn the skills they'll need to achieve their goals throughout life.

8. Recognize and reward effort

It's important to praise children for their accomplishments, but it's also important to let them know you're proud of their efforts regardless of the outcome. It takes hard work to develop new skills, and the results aren't always immediate. Let children know you appreciate the work they're doing, whether they're toddlers building with blocks or teenagers teaching themselves to play the guitar.

9. Expect them to contribute.

Kids may moan, but they feel more connected and appreciated when they are called on to undertake age-appropriate duties, such as tidying up toys, doing dishes, or collecting younger siblings after a play date. Homework and after-school activities are fantastic, but what is needed by your family is priceless.

10. Accept imperfection

As adults, we know that perfection is unattainable, and kids must understand that whether it's on TV, in a magazine, or on a friend's social media feed, the idea that others are always happy, successful, and perfectly dressed is a fantasy, and a destructive one; instead, remind them that being less than perfect is human and completely acceptable.

11. Prepare them for success

Challenges are excellent for kids, but they should also have chances where they may be certain of success. Encourage your child to participate in activities that will help him feel comfortable and secure enough to handle a larger task.

12. Express your feelings

Let your child know you love him regardless of whether he wins or loses the big game, gets good grades or bad grades, or even when you're mad at him. Making sure your child knows you think they're great — and not just when they do great things— will boost their self-esteem even when they're not feeling good about themselves.

Effective Strategies for Raising a Confident Adolescent

Children who appeared confident throughout childhood may struggle to maintain that confidence during adolescence, which for many is a time of self-doubt, a problematic body image, and insecurity.

The good news is that you can take efforts to help your adolescent develop self-esteem, which will benefit your kid in a variety of ways. Teens who have confidence are better equipped to handle peer pressure, negotiate problematic dating situations, make wise decisions, and recover from setbacks.

1. Encourage Self-Improvement

Teens who struggle to grasp a skill may conclude that they are total failures. For example, a teen who struggles with arithmetic may think that they are not clever, and a teen who fails to join the soccer team may conclude that they will never be excellent at sports.

Show your teen that it is acceptable to accept shortcomings while simultaneously working to get better. Rather than labeling themselves as "dumb," help your teen recognize that even if they are suffering intellectually, they can still seek to become better. Help your teen identify their strengths and weaknesses, then engage them in goal setting and problem-solving so they can work toward improving in areas where they struggle. Make sure the goals they set are attainable and within their control, and then map out a plan for how they will achieve those goals.

2. Praise Effort Rather Than Outcome

Instead of complimenting your teen on getting a good grade on an exam, compliment them on all of their studying. Instead of saying, "Great job scoring those five points in the game," say, "All that practicing you've been doing has been paying off." Show them that it's important to try hard and that it's OK if they don't always succeed.

Your teen can control their effort, but they cannot always control the outcome; it is critical to recognize their energy and effort so they do not believe they are only deserving praise when they succeed.

3. Teach Assertiveness Techniques

Teens must learn how to advocate for themselves acceptably.3 An assertive teen will be able to ask for help when they don't grasp school work rather than falling behind. A kid who can speak out is less likely to be treated harshly by classmates because they will speak up for themselves when they don't like how they're being treated and will be able to ask for what they need directly.

To educate your teen to be assertive, first discuss the distinction between being assertive and aggressive, and explain that being assertive involves standing up for yourself with a loud and confident voice without being disrespectful or shouting at others.

Allowing them to make choices and reinforcing that they have rights—especially the right to say no to anything that makes them uncomfortable—are other ways to instill assertiveness skills. Give them ample opportunities to practice their assertiveness skills at home by offering them choices and allowing them the freedom to say no to things they don't want to do.

How Learning to Be Assertive Benefits Children

- Encourage New Possibilities

Adolescents' confidence can increase through trying new hobbies, finding hidden abilities, and challenging themselves, yet many teens are terrified of failure and don't want to disgrace themselves.

Encourage your teen to join a new club, learn to play a musical instrument, volunteer, or find a part-time job. Learning new skills will make them feel better about themselves, and belonging to a group not only provides them with friendship opportunities but can also make them feel more secure and confident.

- Model Self-assurance

Your adolescent will learn the most about confidence from what you do rather than what you say; if you make critical remarks about your physique or talents, you will educate your youngster to do the same.

Model how to face new situations with courage and confidence, as well as the importance of loving yourself.4 Tell your teen about times when you've been brave or things you've done in your life to boost your confidence.

- Create Self-Worth

If your teen only feels good when they receive a certain number of likes on social media or when they fit into a certain size of pants, they will struggle to maintain confidence when situations do not meet their needs. Basing self-worth on superficial things, external circumstances, or other people leads to a lack of confidence in the long run.

Help your kid establish a solid and secure basis for self-worth by emphasizing your beliefs and teaching that genuine self-worth is about living those values; show them that being kind and loving is more important than being slim or attractive.5

- Balance your freedom with your guidance.

Micromanaging your teen's choices will just perpetuate the notion that they can't be trusted to make smart decisions on their own. It's critical to strike the correct mix of independence and advice.

Allow your kids' lots of opportunities to apply the skills you've taught them, and they'll learn from their errors, developing more confidence in their ability to make healthy choices over time.

- Encourage Positive Self-Talk

Your adolescent's inner monologue will have a big impact on how they feel about themselves; if they're always thinking things like, "I'm so unattractive," or "No one likes me," they'll feel horrible about themselves. Teach your kid to establish positive self-talk.
Show them how many of their views are false and how being too harsh may be harmful. Teach them to replace illogical thinking like, "I'm going to fail because I'm stupid," with something more practical like, "I can pass math class if I study hard."

When an adolescent is confident, they can take chances, think outside the box, and pursue their goals in life. Confidence may also help resilience, especially if they are armed with the belief that they will overcome even the most challenging obstacles.

To boost your teen's self-esteem, make confidence-building a regular part of your parenting. Consistently challenge them, encourage them to try new things, and most importantly, believe in themselves even when they fail. Help them set goals and then be their biggest cheerleader, focusing on their hard work rather than the actual results.

If, despite your efforts, your teen continues to struggle with anxiety or shows signs of depression, talk to your doctor about your concerns. Their low self-esteem may be the result of a mental health issue, which, with proper treatment and care, they can overcome and learn to be more confident in the process.

Teaching Healthy Communication Techniques

Possessing a set of proper oral language skills can be described as an essential life skill in today's times. Parents should begin teaching their children basic communication skills during their early years and work to hone those skills as they grow. Assuming that children will learn suitable communication skills without parental guidance is a huge mistake.

What Is the Importance of Communication Skills in Child Development?

Communication skills are essential in the development of children for the following reasons:

- Teaching children effective communication skills allows them to express themselves more clearly and convey their feelings more effectively.

- Communication skills can facilitate learning and meaningful information exchange with others.

- Communication skills can increase your child's social IQ by assisting him in developing good relationships with others.

A youngster who is comfortable generating written communication may be more comfortable producing vocal communication, which will help him perform better academically. Kids with communication impairments may develop behavioral disorders such as sadness, social disengagement, and low self-esteem.

Basic Communication Skills a Child Should Know

Here are some basic communication skills that a child should know:

- Children should be able to create eye contact with the person they are talking to. This is merely a signal of attention and respect. Looking away during a conversation is an indication of indifference, and constitutes bad manners.

- Kids need to learn to communicate appropriately and clearly. Train them to speak using accurate pronunciation and right grammar. It should be urged upon them not to speak rapidly.

- Parents should instruct their kids not to interrupt an ongoing conversation and start talking because they want to. It is essential to check this behavior and encourage self-control.

- Parents need to model good listening conduct, so that youngsters may learn to listen carefully and reply suitably.

- Parents may also show their children the skill of entering a discussion gracefully, and the appropriate way to behave when somebody joins a dynamic conversation, which involves greeting the individual with an encouraging grin and nod.

What to Do if the Child Is Unable to Communicate Effectively

Some useful tips on how to develop children's communication skills can be:

- Build an open line of communication so that your child can easily approach you and express himself without hesitation.

- Let your child have plenty of time to process what he wishes to say, and allow him to finish, to prevent the occurrence of stuttering. Refrain from cutting in or interrupting him while he is trying to respond.

- Avoid overcorrection and being overcritical while teaching your child to speak well. It will only discourage him.

- Children usually learn best by imitating their adults. Therefore, parents should present a good speaking model to their kids to help them communicate suitably.

- When communicating with your child, ensure you take turns, make proper eye contact, and display appreciation for his active participation.

Some Fun Communication Activities and Games for Kids
Some interesting communication activities and games for kids are:

- Play Telephone

This popular and fun game helps enhance good listening skills in kids and can be played by kids of all age groups. You can include other members of the family as well. Have everyone sit in a circle, close enough to whisper easily. Start with one child, who will whisper a message into the ear of the player sitting to the right, who then whispers it into his neighbor's ears, and so on until everyone in the circle has taken a turn. The player at the end relays the message out loud. Once this is done, the last person to receive the message can reveal it. The original message and the final received message will likely differ! You can start with a simple message, and slowly progress to more complex sentences.

- Pointing Directions

Nonverbal communication activities for kids can include this simple game. Ask your kid to write down directions to his nearby favorite shop or park. Then, embark on a journey along with your kid, following those written directions to reach the place. On the way, help him understand how he can make them better, or things he may mention to communicate better.

- Show and Tell

A show and tell activity can be a delightful verbal communication game for kids. Give your kid a topic, like his favorite fruit, a favorite book, or a road trip with the family. Have him exhibit an item related to the topic, and ask him to speak five lines on it. This activity can assist in furthering your kid's confidence, vocabulary, and eloquence.

- Picture Storytelling

Picture storytelling can be an exciting activity, as kids love to tell stories. Provide your kid with a set of pictures. Ask him to arrange them in a logical sequence and spin a story from it. Alternatively, you can offer him just one picture, and have him describe the things he perceives in the picture, like the scenery, people, colors, and other details.

- Presentation

This exciting activity will not only promote your kid's oral language skills but will also help him get comfortable with public speaking. You can propose various themes, ranging from the recitation of a favorite poem to expressing his views on current topics like saving water, recycling, the use of gadgets, and so on. Ask him to prepare a short presentation to present to a family gathering, local park functions, or anywhere he feels comfortable.

- Extempore

Extempore or spontaneous speech forms an integral part of oral communication and can be used to expand communication skills. Extempore helps support your kid in thinking on his feet and articulating his ideas correctly. This activity will suitably prepare him for future career prospects as well. Make chits on interesting topics, and have your kid pick a chit and speak on the chosen topic, impromptu, for a few minutes.

- Emotional Charades

This fun activity is great for helping kids understand different facial expressions, signals, and body postures when communicating. These are the non-verbal communication cues that complement verbal communication. Hand out a few cards to your kid, each card depicting a particular emotion or feeling, like anger, sadness, boredom, fatigue, or happiness, and have him act them out. Your kids can also draw the different emotions he is likely to experience in ordinary situations.

- 20 Questions

20 questions is a wonderful game that enables your kid's ability to formulate and ask direct questions. Ask kids to stand in a circle. Let one kid stand in the center, and he has to think of a famous place or a known personality. The other kids in the group have to identify it by asking a set of 20 questions. The child can respond by saying only yes or no. In case the group fails to guess, the child in the center is declared the winner!

- Identify the Object

You may require 4 -5 kids to play this game. Blindfold one child, while the rest of the players choose an object that can be described elaborately for easy identification. Every player takes a turn describing one feature of the selected object. The blindfolded kid may ask additional questions as cues.

- Changing the Leader

This game can be a great training tool for teaching kids how to recognize body language indicators. Choose one kid as the leader, who will perform specific actions, like stomping his feet or clapping. The other kids have to imitate his actions. The leader then selects another kid as the leader by smiling or winking at him. Other kids have to detect the new leader and then replicate his actions.

Parents who communicate often and efficiently with their kids may be able to help them develop sound communication skills easily. Communication proficiency may not only provide your kid with better comfort in social situations but can also ensure improved performance academically and later in their careers.

5 Effective Methods for Teaching Kids Communication Skills

Effective communication is a key life skill, and we need to help our children as they develop their communication skills from an early age. The way a child can communicate impacts the process of learning and the meaningful exchange of information. A child who can communicate his or her thoughts, feelings, and ideas in a classroom setting is more likely to perform better at school than a student who does not communicate effectively. Children with strong communication skills are also more likely to build healthy relationships with others as they encounter more opportunities to socialize with peers because they are better equipped to express themselves and convey their feelings more effectively.

Just like with any other skill, your child's communication skills can be improved with practice, and there are several approaches you may find helpful as a parent to help your child. Here's a list of tips you can use to help your child develop strong communication skills.

- Encourage conversation as often as possible

As a parent, you need to encourage your child to begin or join in on conversations as much as possible. We know that as children develop and grow, they learn how to socialize by practicing their burgeoning conversational skills, as they observe what works for them in different situations. But did you know that it's also important for adults, especially parents, to help kids practice these skills?

Start with casual conversations, such as the ones you may have while preparing a meal together or during a car ride. If you're in the car together, you may chat about where you're going, discuss the destination, and ask your child how he or she is feeling. If you're working together in the kitchen, you can encourage conversation by talking about the recipe and the steps involved. Engage by answering your child's questions, especially if you get the sense that your child is enthusiastic about being involved.

- Listen to whitelisted to what your child has to say

Listening is also a vital skill for kids to learn at an early age. A great way to teach your child about the importance of good listening skills is by modeling this behavior yourself. Active listening skills start with you as a parent setting an example for your child. When children are repeating what you say and mimicking your actions, it shows that repetition reinforces the behavior we want our children to learn. We see this when we teach our kids about manners or how to act in social interactions (for example, saying "Hello" back to someone.

You can model good listening skills by paying attention to what your child says. Repeat back part of what your child has said to confirm your understanding. It's also a good idea to follow up with a question. For example, you may say, "It looks like you had a great time during your art session. What kind of project do you plan to work on next time?"

- Make conversations fun

Another tip for teaching good communication skills to kids is to incorporate fun into conversations. There are days when it may feel challenging to come up with interesting topics. You can start by sharing a funny story or experience you had during the day. Then, encourage your child to share their own funny stories or talk about activities they did at school.

- Read with your child

Reading skills are an essential aspect of effective communication and overall language development. Reading skills benefit children in so many ways, including teaching new words, expanding their vocabulary, and enhancing their cognitive abilities.

Research also shows that children who read regularly tend to be more empathetic toward others than children without exposure to the written word. When kids read, it

..s them to experience the joy and pain of others through stories.

- Teach children how to take turns

Because listening is part of effective communication, it's important to teach your child how to wait for his or her turn to speak. You can practice this by using toys or playing games. For example, you may play a game in which the person holds the ball when it's his or her turn to speak. Your child then waits for the ball to be passed to him or her before speaking.

Good communication skills aren't something that children are born with. This is where your role as parents comes in. Follow these tips to help you teach your child about communication skills so he or she can be better equipped for success in school, and beyond.

Thank you❁

Check out other works by the author:

Queening Mindfully Floral Womens Coloring Book
https://www.amazon.com/dp/B0BFV63P1C

Blooming Queen Anxiety Relief Botanical Coloring Book
https://www.amazon.com/dp/B0BF2XK8F7

Haunted Nights Halloween Coloring Book
https://www.amazon.com/dp/B0BF2XBDFL

Black Girl Badass Notebook
https://www.amazon.com/dp/B0BFFYVJB9

Paper Bound Adventure Creative Journal for Young Readers
https://www.amazon.com/dp/B0B9QPW3PD

There are so much more creative, inspirational and helpful books on our Amazon page, we hope to see you soon!

www.ingramcontent.com/pod-product-compliance
Lightning Source LLC
LaVergne TN
LVHW082247150826
845677LV00009B/1556

9798354854127